Pharma 4.0
The Digital Transformation Blueprint

Dr. Jayant Joshi

DR. JAYANT JOSHI

PHARMA 4.0

THE DIGITAL TRANSFORMATION
BLUEPRINT

2025

WWW.RESPA.COM

Table of Contents

Introduction.. *1*

Pharma 4.0 Overview 3
Industry context and drivers for digital transformation...................................5

Digital Transformation in Pharma 7
Challenges and opportunities in the pharmaceutical industry 7
Role of Technology in overcoming traditional manufacturing challenges 10

Part 1: Core Technologies of Pharma 4.0 ....*13*

Artificial Intelligence (AI) in Pharma............................... 14
Applications of AI in drug discovery and manufacturing............................. 14
AI-driven Quality Control and Predictive Maintenance............................... 16

Internet of Things (IoT) and Smart Manufacturing...................... 18
IoT Applications in Real-Time Monitoring and Automation........................... 18
Case studies of IoT implementation in Pharmaceutical Smart Manufacturing20

Big Data Analytics and Machine Learning........................... 22
Leveraging Data Analytics for Process Optimization 22
Machine Learning Applications in Predictive Modelling............................... 24

Cloud Computing and Cybersecurity 26
Cloud-Based Solutions for Data Management and Collaboration................. 26
Cybersecurity Strategies for Protecting Sensitive Data............................... 29

Part 2: Implementation and Benefits *31*

Digital Transformation Strategies for Pharma 32
Change Management and Organizational Readiness................................... 32
Building a Digital Culture within Pharmaceutical Companies....................... 34

Enhancing Operational Efficiency..................................... 36
Streamlining Production Processes with Automation 36
Reducing Costs and Improving Productivity 38

Quality Control and Compliance 40
Using Digital Tools for Regulatory Compliance 40
Ensuring Data Integrity and Traceability 42

Personalized Medicine and Patient-Centric Approaches................. 44
Role of Pharma 4.0 in Personalized Medicine 44
Patient-Centric Innovations enabled by Digital Technologies 46

Part 3: Future Directions and Challenges *49*

Future Trends in Pharma 4.0 .... **50**
Emerging Technologies like Blockchain and 3D Printing 50
Potential Impact on Drug Development and Manufacturing 53

Challenges and Limitations **55**
Addressing Regulatory Hurdles and Cybersecurity Risks 55
Overcoming Cultural and Technological Barriers 57

Case Studies and Success Stories **59**
Real-world examples of Pharma 4.0 implementation 59
Lessons learned from early adopters 60

Conclusion *63*

Pharma 4.0: The Road Ahead **64**
Vision for the Future of Pharmaceutical Manufacturing 64
Call to Action for Industry Stakeholders 66

Appendix *69*

Glossary of key terms **70**

Resources for further learning **72**

About the Author *73*

Introduction

Pharma 4.0 Overview

Definition and evolution of Pharma 4.0

Pharma 4.0 is an extension of Industry 4.0, specifically tailored for the pharmaceutical industry. It involves the integration of advanced digital technologies such as Artificial Intelligence (AI), the Internet of Things (IoT), Big Data Analytics, and Cloud Computing to enhance manufacturing processes.

Definition of Pharma 4.0

Pharma 4.0 is a framework developed by the International Society for Pharmaceutical Engineering (ISPE) to modernize pharmaceutical manufacturing. It leverages Industry 4.0 principles to improve efficiency, quality, and responsiveness in the pharmaceutical sector.

Evolution of Pharma 4.0

The concept of Pharma 4.0 emerged as a response to the challenges faced by the pharmaceutical industry, such as high development costs, lengthy timelines, and regulatory hurdles. It was formally introduced in 2017 to apply Industry 4.0 technologies to pharmaceutical development and production.

Key Components and Technologies

1. Artificial Intelligence (AI): Used for predictive maintenance, quality control, and optimizing production processes.

2. Internet of Things (IoT): Enables real-time monitoring and control of manufacturing conditions.
3. Big Data Analytics: Analyzes large datasets to extract insights for process optimization.
4. Cloud Computing: Facilitates data management and collaboration across departments.
5. Robotics and Automation: Streamlines manufacturing processes and reduces human intervention.
6. Blockchain: Enhances supply chain transparency and security.

Benefits of Pharma 4.0

- Improved Manufacturing Efficiency: Real-time monitoring and automation reduce downtime and increase productivity.
- Enhanced Quality Control: Early detection of quality issues ensures consistent product quality.
- Personalized Medicine: Enables tailored treatments through advanced data analysis.
- Supply Chain Management: Real-time tracking improves inventory management and distribution.
- Patient Safety: Ensures safer, high-quality products.

Challenges and Future Outlook

Implementing Pharma 4.0 requires addressing regulatory complexities, ensuring cybersecurity, and fostering a digital culture. As technology continues to evolve, Pharma 4.0 is poised to revolutionize the pharmaceutical industry by accelerating drug development, improving manufacturing efficiency, and enhancing patient outcomes.

Industry context and drivers for digital transformation

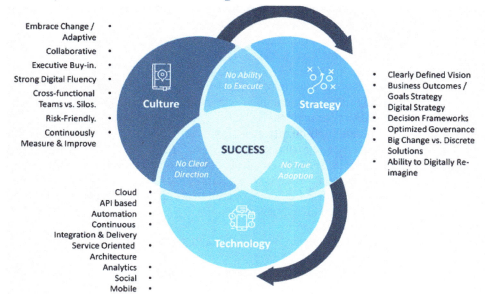

- Embrace Change / Adaptive
- Collaborative
- Executive Buy-in.
- Strong Digital Fluency
- Cross-functional Teams vs. Silos.
- Risk-Friendly.
- Continuously Measure & Improve

Culture

No Ability to Execute

Strategy

- Clearly Defined Vision
- Business Outcomes / Goals Strategy
- Digital Strategy
- Decision Frameworks
- Optimized Governance
- Big Change vs. Discrete Solutions
- Ability to Digitally Re-imagine

SUCCESS

No Clear Direction

No True Adoption

- Cloud
- API based
- Automation
- Continuous Integration & Delivery
- Service Oriented Architecture
- Analytics
- Social
- Mobile

Technology

The pharmaceutical industry is undergoing significant digital transformation driven by several key factors:

Industry Context

- Global Market Growth: The pharmaceutical market is expected to reach $1,565.5 billion by 2028, with a growing demand for innovative treatments and personalized medicine.
- Regulatory Pressures: Increasing regulatory scrutiny and the need for compliance with evolving standards like GDPR and HIPAA.
- Patient Expectations: Patients now expect more personalized and accessible healthcare solutions, driving the need for digital platforms and data-driven insights.

Drivers for Digital Transformation

1. Technological Advancements:
    - AI and Machine Learning: Enhance drug discovery, predict outcomes, and optimize clinical trials.
    - Cloud Computing: Enables scalable data management and analysis.
    - IoT and Wearable Devices: Provide real-time patient data for personalized treatment plans.

5

2. Operational Efficiency:
   o Automation and Digitalization: Streamline manufacturing processes, reduce waste, and improve productivity.
   o Faster Time-to-Market: Accelerate R&D and clinical trials through digital tools.
3. Quality and Compliance:
   o Regulatory Requirements: Ensure data integrity and traceability while navigating complex regulatory environments.
   o Quality Management Systems: Use real-time monitoring to maintain high-quality standards.
4. Patient-Centricity and Sustainability:
   o Personalized Medicine: Tailor treatments to individual needs using advanced data analytics.
   o Sustainability: Implement green manufacturing practices to meet environmental responsibilities.
5. Challenges and Pain Points:
   o Legacy Systems: Overcoming outdated infrastructure and high upgrade costs.
   o Data Management: Addressing data silos and security concerns.

These drivers and challenges highlight the necessity for pharmaceutical companies to embrace digital transformation to remain competitive, efficient, and compliant in a rapidly evolving industry landscape.

Digital Transformation in Pharma

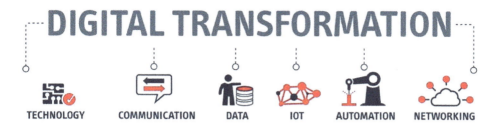

Challenges and opportunities in the pharmaceutical industry

The pharmaceutical industry is facing numerous challenges and opportunities as it navigates a complex landscape of technological advancements, regulatory pressures, and global health demands. Here's an overview of these challenges and opportunities:

Challenges

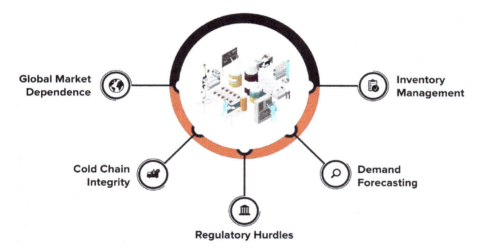

1. Rising Operational Complexity:
   - The industry faces increased operational complexity due to new modalities like cell and gene therapy, which require specialized manufacturing processes and supply chains.
   - Regulatory compliance and data management become more intricate with these advancements.

7

2. Supply Chain Pressures:
   o Supply chain disruptions can lead to significant losses; the pharma industry is somewhat protected but still vulnerable to global supply chain pressures.
   o Inflation and rising costs for raw materials and transportation add to these challenges.
3. Talent Shortages:
   o The industry is experiencing talent shortages, particularly in digital and STEM roles, which are crucial for leveraging emerging technologies.
   o Remote work trends have increased employee expectations for flexibility, complicating talent management.
4. Regulatory Compliance:
   o Pharmaceutical companies must navigate complex regulatory environments, including evolving standards for clinical trials and product approvals.
   o Failure to comply can result in costly fines and reputational damage.
5. Pricing Pressures:
   o Companies face increasing pressure to control product costs due to government regulations and consumer demands.
   o This pressure can limit investment in R&D and new product development.
6. Intellectual Property and Patent Expirations:
   o The industry relies heavily on patents, which provide limited exclusivity. Generic competition after patent expiration can significantly impact sales and revenue.
   o The looming patent cliff is expected to drive mergers and acquisitions in 2025.

Opportunities

1. Digital Transformation:
   o The advancement of digital tools, AI, and analytics offers opportunities for increased efficiency, better decision-making, and enhanced patient outcomes.
   o Technologies like edge computing and cloud analytics provide real-time optimization and transparency.
2. AI-Powered Drug Discovery:
   o AI accelerates drug discovery, optimizes clinical trial design, and identifies biomarkers more efficiently.
   o This can lead to faster development of new treatments and improved success rates in drug development.

3. Personalized Medicine:
   o Advances in genomics and biotechnology are making personalized medicine more mainstream, offering tailored treatments for patients.
   o This approach can improve patient outcomes and enhance the effectiveness of treatments.
4. Expansion of mRNA Technology:
   o The success of mRNA vaccines during the COVID-19 pandemic has opened new avenues for this technology, potentially leading to breakthroughs in other disease areas.
   o mRNA technology offers rapid development and production capabilities, which can be crucial in responding to future pandemics.
5. Sustainability Initiatives:
   o Pharmaceutical companies are under pressure to adopt sustainable practices, which can lead to cost savings and improved public perception.
   o Initiatives like waste reduction and green manufacturing can enhance operational efficiency while meeting environmental responsibilities.
6. Global Health Equity Initiatives:
   o Efforts to address disparities in healthcare access are gaining momentum, with pharma companies playing a crucial role in improving global health equity.
   o These initiatives can enhance patient access to essential treatments and improve health outcomes worldwide.

In summary, while the pharmaceutical industry faces significant challenges, it also has opportunities to leverage technological advancements, improve operational efficiency, and enhance patient care through innovative strategies and partnerships.

Role of Technology in overcoming traditional manufacturing challenges

Technology plays a pivotal role in overcoming traditional manufacturing challenges in the pharmaceutical industry. Here are some ways technology addresses these challenges:

Addressing Traditional Challenges

1. Regulatory Compliance:
   o Cloud-Based Solutions: Ensure data accessibility, accuracy, and compliance with regulatory requirements like FDA standards. These systems build compliance into the manufacturing process, reducing audit failures due to outdated or incorrectly documented procedures.
   o Automated Quality Assurance: AI and machine learning help maintain high-quality standards by detecting anomalies early, ensuring regulatory compliance and reducing the risk of costly recalls.
2. Information Silos:
   o Integrated MES and LES Systems: These systems ensure that all teams involved in drug production are on the same platform, eliminating information silos and enhancing collaboration across departments.
   o Cloud Computing: Facilitates real-time data sharing and collaboration, reducing the risk of data miscommunication and improving supply chain visibility.

3. Knowledge Gaps:
    o Digital Knowledge Management: Modern solutions optimize the transfer of knowledge, ensuring that manufacturing processes are not dependent on individual expertise. This reduces the risk of process interruptions when key personnel are unavailable.
    o AI-Driven Insights: Analyze large datasets to identify best practices and optimize processes, reducing reliance on individual knowledge.
4. Process Inflexibility:
    o No-Code and Low-Code Solutions: Allow users to configure and adapt manufacturing processes without needing extensive IT support, enhancing flexibility and reducing development time.
    o Modular Manufacturing: Enables greater flexibility in production, especially for complex modalities like cell and gene therapies, by focusing on product attributes rather than fixed processes.
5. Lack of Real-Time Visibility:
    o IoT and Real-Time Monitoring: Provide instant visibility across manufacturing operations, allowing for quick identification and resolution of quality issues.
    o Digital Twins: Simulate manufacturing processes to optimize production and predict potential bottlenecks before they occur.
6. Human Error:
    o Automation and Robotics: Reduce the need for human intervention, minimizing errors and enhancing safety in hazardous environments.
    o Augmented Reality (AR) Technologies: Digitally manage procedures to reduce misinterpretation and ensure precise execution of tasks.

Future Outlook

As technology continues to evolve, pharmaceutical manufacturing will see increased adoption of AI, IoT, and automation. These technologies will further enhance efficiency, quality, and compliance, enabling faster development and delivery of innovative treatments to patients. Modular manufacturing and digital twins will play crucial roles in optimizing production processes for complex therapies, ensuring that the industry remains agile and responsive to changing healthcare needs.

Part 1: Core Technologies of Pharma 4.0

Artificial Intelligence (AI) in Pharma

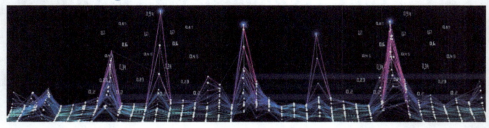

Applications of AI in drug discovery and manufacturing

Artificial Intelligence (AI) is transforming drug manufacturing by enhancing efficiency, quality, and compliance across various stages of production. Here are some key applications of AI in drug manufacturing:

Applications of AI in Drug Manufacturing

1. Quality Control and Assurance:
   - AI uses advanced image recognition and data analysis to detect deviations in real-time, ensuring products meet stringent regulatory standards.
   - AI supports identifying root causes of deviations and suggests corrective actions (CAPAs) by recognizing deviation patterns.
2. Process Monitoring and Fault Detection:
   - AI enhances process monitoring by analyzing real-time data from manufacturing equipment, allowing for early identification of potential issues and reducing downtime.
   - Predictive maintenance minimizes equipment failures, maintaining production efficiency.
3. Yield and Output Optimization:
   - AI optimizes production processes to improve batch yields and reduce waste.
   - Predictive process monitoring allows for real-time adjustments to maintain optimal production conditions.
4. Flexible Manufacturing and Supply Chain Management:
   - AI forecasts demand and optimizes inventory levels, enhancing supply chain transparency and efficiency.
   - Real-time monitoring ensures that drugs are available when needed, reducing stockouts and overstocking.

5. Generative AI in Manufacturing:
    o Companies like Pfizer use generative AI platforms to detect anomalies and suggest real-time actions to operators, boosting product yield and reducing cycle times.
    o AI algorithms can generate synthesis pathways for drug compounds, improving manufacturing efficiency.

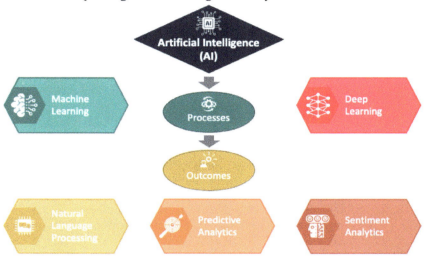

Benefits of AI in Drug Manufacturing

- Faster Production Times: AI optimizes processes, reducing production cycle times and enabling faster delivery of medicines to patients.
- Lower Costs: AI reduces waste and improves efficiency, leading to cost savings in manufacturing.
- Higher Quality Products: Enhanced quality control ensures consistent product quality, reducing the risk of recalls.
- Regulatory Compliance: AI supports adherence to regulatory standards by providing transparent and traceable data throughout the manufacturing process.

By leveraging these AI applications, pharmaceutical companies can significantly enhance their manufacturing capabilities, improve product quality, and accelerate the delivery of life-saving treatments to patients.

AI-driven Quality Control and Predictive Maintenance

| Data Collection | Data Analysis | Quality Prediction | Quality Prediction | Continuous Improvement |

AI-driven quality control and predictive maintenance are transforming the pharmaceutical industry by enhancing efficiency, reducing downtime, and ensuring compliance with regulatory standards. Here's how AI is impacting these areas:

AI-Driven Quality Control

1. Automated Inspection:
   - AI-powered computer vision systems analyze images to detect defects in product appearance, labels, or packaging, ensuring consistent visual quality standards.
   - Real-time monitoring of critical quality parameters like temperature, humidity, and pressure ensures that they remain within acceptable ranges.
2. Data Analysis and Pattern Recognition:
   - AI analyzes large volumes of data from quality control tests, environmental monitoring, and batch records to quickly identify patterns or anomalies, detecting quality issues faster than manual methods.
   - AI enhances the validation of analytical methods, leading to higher accuracy and precision in test results.
3. Root Cause Analysis:
   - AI algorithms perform root cause analysis by examining complex data sets to identify factors contributing to quality issues, helping to implement corrective actions and prevent future deviations.

Predictive Maintenance

1. Equipment Monitoring:
   - AI uses real-time data from equipment sensors to predict potential failures, allowing for proactive maintenance scheduling and minimizing unexpected downtime.
   - Predictive analytics detect early signs of wear and tear in machinery, enabling timely interventions before failures occur.

2. Reduced Downtime and Costs:
    o By predicting equipment failures, AI helps schedule repairs in advance, reducing downtime and saving costs associated with emergency repairs and unnecessary maintenance.
    o Predictive maintenance extends the lifespan of equipment, reducing the need for expensive replacements.
3. Improved Product Quality:
    o Well-maintained machines ensure consistent production quality, reducing defects and ensuring medicines meet safety standards.
    o AI supports maintaining stable environmental conditions in clean rooms, preventing product contamination due to faulty systems.

Benefits and Challenges

- Benefits: Enhanced quality control, reduced downtime, improved product consistency, and cost savings.
- Challenges: Requires high-quality data, specialized expertise, and robust infrastructure to implement effectively.

By leveraging AI in quality control and predictive maintenance, pharmaceutical companies can significantly enhance operational efficiency, improve product quality, and ensure regulatory compliance, ultimately contributing to better patient outcomes.

Internet of Things (IoT) and Smart Manufacturing

IoT Applications in Real-Time Monitoring and Automation

IoT applications in real-time monitoring and automation are transforming the pharmaceutical industry by enhancing efficiency, quality, and compliance across various stages of production and distribution. Here's an overview of how IoT is applied in these areas:

1. Equipment Performance Monitoring:
   o IoT sensors continuously monitor equipment performance in real-time, tracking parameters like temperature, vibration, and pressure.
   o This monitoring allows for early detection of anomalies, enabling proactive maintenance and reducing downtime.
2. Environmental Control:
   o IoT devices ensure that manufacturing environments remain within specified conditions (e.g., temperature, humidity) to maintain product quality.
   o Real-time adjustments can be made to prevent deviations that might affect product integrity.
3. Supply Chain Visibility:
   o IoT technologies like RFID tags and GPS provide real-time tracking of products throughout the supply chain.
   o This visibility enhances inventory management, reduces delays, and ensures compliance with regulatory standards.

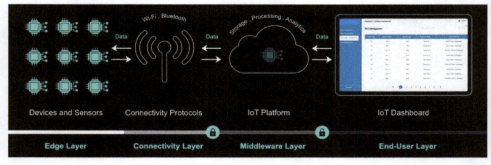

IoT Applications in Automation

1. Predictive Maintenance:
   o IoT data is analyzed using predictive algorithms to forecast equipment failures before they occur.
   o This proactive approach minimizes unplanned downtime and extends equipment lifespan.
2. Automated Quality Control:
   o IoT sensors automate quality checks by continuously monitoring production parameters, ensuring consistent product quality.
   o Automated systems can intervene early to correct deviations, reducing the risk of defective products.
3. Smart Manufacturing Systems:
   o IoT integrates with automation systems to optimize production workflows, reducing manual errors and improving efficiency.
   o Real-time data enables swift decision-making and adjustments to maintain optimal production conditions.

Benefits of IoT in Real-Time Monitoring and Automation

- Improved Efficiency: Reduced downtime and optimized production processes enhance overall efficiency.
- Enhanced Quality: Real-time monitoring ensures consistent product quality and compliance with regulatory standards.
- Increased Transparency: IoT provides end-to-end visibility across the supply chain, improving inventory management and reducing risks.
- Cost Savings: Predictive maintenance and reduced waste lead to significant cost savings.

By leveraging IoT for real-time monitoring and automation, pharmaceutical companies can achieve greater operational efficiency, improve product quality, and enhance supply chain resilience, ultimately contributing to better patient outcomes.

Case studies of IoT implementation in Pharmaceutical Smart Manufacturing

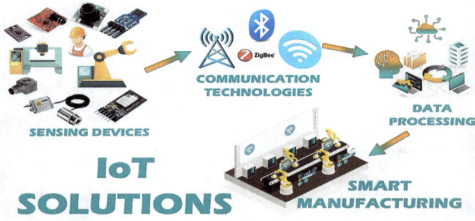

Here are some case studies and examples of IoT implementation in pharmaceutical manufacturing:

1. Pfizer's Smart Manufacturing:
   - Pfizer uses IoT sensors to monitor production processes in real-time, ensuring that each batch meets stringent quality requirements.
   - This approach enhances efficiency and compliance, allowing for swift adjustments to maintain optimal production conditions.
2. Novartis and Predictive Analytics:
   - Novartis leverages IoT-enabled predictive analytics to monitor equipment performance and prevent unplanned downtimes.
   - This proactive approach has improved productivity, reduced costs, and enhanced the delivery of high-quality products.
3. Roche's Digital Transformation:
   - Roche has adopted IoT technologies to streamline manufacturing processes, ensuring regulatory compliance and quality standards.
   - IoT devices monitor production parameters, demonstrating the transformative potential of IoT in the pharma industry.
4. IoT-Integrated Drug Delivery System:
   - A pioneering project developed an IoT-integrated drug delivery system that enhances real-time monitoring and administration, improving patient care.
   - The system uses IoT devices connected to patients, providing real-time updates on drug delivery status and potential errors.
5. Merck's BrightLab Program:
   - Merck introduced BrightLab, a cloud program leveraging IoT for research and development efficiency.
   - This program enhances inventory and instrument management, improving supply chain operations.

Key Benefits Observed

- Improved Efficiency: IoT optimizes production processes, reducing waste and enhancing productivity.
- Enhanced Quality: Real-time monitoring ensures consistent product quality and compliance with regulatory standards.
- Increased Transparency: IoT provides visibility across the supply chain, facilitating better inventory management and demand forecasting.
- Cost Savings: Predictive maintenance and reduced waste lead to significant cost savings.

These case studies highlight how IoT is transforming pharmaceutical manufacturing by enhancing efficiency, quality, and compliance while improving patient outcomes.

Big Data Analytics and Machine Learning

Leveraging Data Analytics for Process Optimization

Leveraging data analytics for process optimization in pharmaceutical manufacturing involves using advanced analytics tools to analyze large datasets and extract actionable insights. This approach enhances efficiency, quality, and compliance across various stages of production. Here's how data analytics contributes to process optimization:

Key Applications of Data Analytics in Process Optimization

1. Predictive Maintenance:
    o Equipment Monitoring: Data analytics helps predict equipment failures by analyzing sensor data, allowing for proactive maintenance scheduling and minimizing unplanned downtime.
    o Reduced Downtime: By anticipating potential issues, companies can reduce downtime and maintain consistent production levels.
2. Process Optimization:
    o Efficiency Improvements: Advanced analytics identifies bottlenecks and inefficiencies in production processes, enabling adjustments to optimize resource utilization and improve productivity.
    o Quality Control: Real-time monitoring detects deviations early, ensuring consistent product quality and compliance with regulatory standards.
3. Supply Chain Optimization:
    o Demand Forecasting: Data analytics predicts demand fluctuations based on historical data and market trends, optimizing inventory levels and reducing stockouts or overstocking.
    o Logistics Improvement: Real-time tracking of shipments and inventory levels minimizes supply chain disruptions and ensures timely delivery of critical medications.

4. Clinical Trials Optimization:
   o Patient Stratification: Analytics helps identify suitable patient populations for clinical trials, improving trial efficiency and reducing costs.
   o Predictive Modeling: Models forecast trial outcomes and patient responses, guiding trial design and optimizing participant selection.

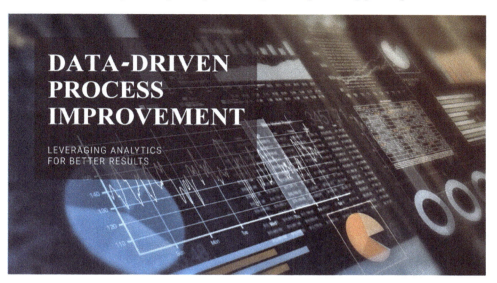

Benefits of Data Analytics in Process Optimization

- Improved Efficiency: Analytics-driven insights streamline production processes, reducing waste and enhancing productivity.
- Enhanced Quality: Real-time monitoring ensures consistent product quality and compliance with regulatory standards.
- Cost Savings: Predictive maintenance and optimized processes reduce operational costs and minimize downtime.
- Better Decision-Making: Data-driven insights support strategic decisions, enabling proactive management of production and supply chain operations.

By leveraging data analytics, pharmaceutical companies can optimize manufacturing processes, improve product quality, and enhance operational efficiency, ultimately contributing to better patient outcomes and improved business performance.

Machine Learning Applications in Predictive Modelling

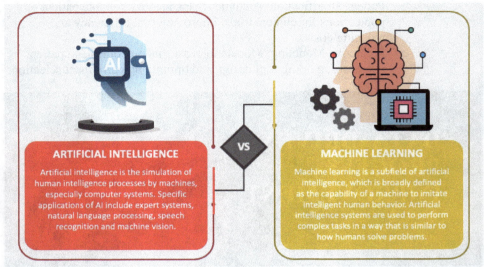

Machine learning (ML) plays a crucial role in predictive modelling by enhancing the accuracy and efficiency of predictions. Here's an overview of how ML is applied in predictive modelling:

Machine Learning in Predictive Modelling

1. Pattern Recognition and Trend Analysis:
   - ML algorithms analyze historical data to identify complex patterns and trends that may not be apparent through traditional statistical methods.
   - This capability allows for more accurate forecasting of future events or outcomes.
2. Automated Decision-Making:
   - ML models can automate decision-making processes by analyzing large datasets and making predictions based on learned patterns.
   - This automation is particularly useful in applications like fraud detection, where real-time analysis is critical.
3. Adaptability and Scalability:
   - ML models can adapt to changing data patterns over time, improving their accuracy as more data becomes available.
   - They can handle large datasets and complex problems, making them scalable for various applications.

Key Machine Learning Algorithms for Predictive Modelling

1. Linear Regression:
   o Used for predicting continuous outcomes based on linear relationships between variables.
   o Commonly applied in forecasting sales or revenue.
2. Decision Trees and Random Forests:
   o Decision trees are used for classification and regression tasks, providing clear visual representations of decision paths.
   o Random forests combine multiple decision trees to improve accuracy and avoid overfitting.
3. Neural Networks:
   o Effective for handling complex, nonlinear relationships in data.
   o Often used in applications like image recognition and speech processing.
4. Support Vector Machines (SVMs):
   o Used for classification tasks by finding the best decision boundary between classes.
   o Effective in applications like text classification and image recognition.

Applications of Machine Learning in Predictive Modelling

1. Financial Services:
   o Credit scoring and risk assessment to predict loan defaults.
   o Fraud detection in transactions.
2. Healthcare:
   o Predicting disease outbreaks and identifying high-risk patients.
   o Personalized treatment recommendations based on patient data.
3. Manufacturing:
   o Predictive maintenance to forecast equipment failures.
   o Quality control by detecting anomalies in production processes.
4. Retail:
   o Customer segmentation and personalized product recommendations.
   o Sales forecasting and inventory management.

By leveraging machine learning in predictive modelling, organizations can make more accurate predictions, automate decision-making processes, and improve operational efficiency across various industries.

Cloud Computing and Cybersecurity

Cloud-Based Solutions for Data Management and Collaboration

Cloud-based solutions for data management and collaboration are transforming the pharmaceutical industry by enhancing efficiency, scalability, and compliance across various stages of drug development and manufacturing. Here's an overview of how cloud technologies support data management and collaboration:

Benefits of Cloud-Based Solutions

1. Scalability and Flexibility:
   - Cloud platforms provide virtually unlimited storage and processing power, allowing companies to scale resources up or down based on project needs.
   - This flexibility is particularly beneficial for managing large datasets and supporting collaborative research projects.
2. Enhanced Collaboration:
   - Cloud environments enable real-time collaboration across global teams, facilitating faster drug development and manufacturing processes.
   - Tools like Google Workspace and Cflow offer features for seamless teamwork, secure file sharing, and centralized workflows.
3. Data Security and Compliance:
   - Reputable cloud service providers offer continuous security monitoring and incident response, ensuring data safety and regulatory compliance.
   - Platforms like Scispot and LabVantage ensure compliance with FDA, HIPAA, GxP, and ISO standards, providing real-time traceability for data integrity.
4. Advanced Analytics and AI Integration:
   - Cloud platforms integrate with AI and machine learning tools, enabling advanced data analysis and insights that can accelerate drug discovery and development.
   - Solutions like Axtria DataMAx facilitate the rapid integration of structured and unstructured data sources, providing actionable business insights.

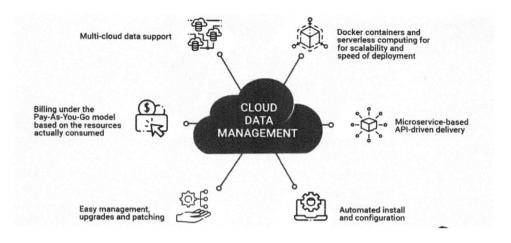

Multi-cloud data support

Docker containers and serverless computing for for scalability and speed of deployment

Billing under the Pay-As-You-Go model based on the resources actually consumed

CLOUD DATA MANAGEMENT

Microservice-based API-driven delivery

Easy management, upgrades and patching

Automated install and configuration

Key Cloud-Based Data Management Tools

1. Microsoft Azure:
   o Offers a range of data management services, including SQL databases, blob storage, and real-time data analysis tools like Azure Data Explorer.
   o Supports multiple database styles and integrates well with other data management tools.
2. Google Cloud Platform:
   o Provides tools like BigQuery for data storage and analytics, Cloud BigTable for NoSQL databases, and ML Engine for advanced machine learning applications.
   o Facilitates seamless integration with standard BI tools for comprehensive data analysis.
3. Fivetran:
   o A fully-managed data pipeline that integrates data from various sources into a single data warehouse, enhancing data centralization and KPI tracking.
   o Offers a sophisticated caching layer for secure data transfer without storing copies on application servers.
4. BC Platforms' Trusted Collaboration Environment (TCE):
   o Enables secure, global collaboration using real-world data to accelerate drug development.
   o Supports diverse datasets and provides a comprehensive view of patient experiences, enhancing study design and safety assessments.

Collaboration Platforms

1. Cflow:
   - Offers workflow automation and team management features, enhancing cloud collaboration with a user-friendly interface.
   - Supports mobile accessibility and integrates well with other business tools.
2. Google Workspace:
   - Provides real-time co-editing capabilities, secure file sharing, and built-in video conferencing tools.
   - Ideal for businesses seeking centralized and secure collaboration solutions.

By leveraging these cloud-based solutions, pharmaceutical companies can streamline data management, enhance collaboration, and accelerate innovation while ensuring regulatory compliance and data security.

Cybersecurity Strategies for Protecting Sensitive Data

Protecting sensitive data in the pharmaceutical industry requires robust cybersecurity strategies that address the unique challenges and regulatory requirements of this sector. Here are some key strategies for safeguarding sensitive data:

Cybersecurity Strategies for Protecting Sensitive Data

1. Implement Advanced Encryption Protocols:
   - Encrypt data both at rest and in transit using strong encryption algorithms like AES or RSA to prevent unauthorized access.
   - Ensure encryption keys are securely managed to maintain data confidentiality.
2. Access Controls and Authentication:
   - Use role-based access control (RBAC) to limit data access to authorized personnel only.
   - Implement multi-factor authentication (MFA) to add an extra layer of security against unauthorized access.
3. Regular Security Audits and Penetration Testing:
   - Conduct regular security audits to identify vulnerabilities and ensure compliance with regulatory standards.
   - Perform penetration testing to simulate cyberattacks and rectify weaknesses before they can be exploited.
4. Incident Response Plan:
   - Develop a comprehensive incident response plan to address cybersecurity incidents effectively, including steps for containment, eradication, recovery, and communication.

29

5. Employee Training and Awareness:
   o Provide regular training to employees on cybersecurity best practices, recognizing phishing attempts, and reporting security incidents.
   o Foster a culture of security awareness to prevent human error-related breaches.
6. Privileged Access Management (PAM):
   o Implement PAM to control and monitor privileged accounts closely, enforcing strict access rules and tracking activities.
7. Endpoint Security:
   o Secure endpoints like laptops and smartphones with antivirus software, firewalls, and device encryption to prevent unauthorized access.
   o Use endpoint detection and response (EDR) solutions to detect and respond to threats in real-time.
8. Data Governance Frameworks:
   o Establish clear data governance policies that define how sensitive data should be handled, accessed, and shared.
   o Regularly review and update these policies to align with industry best practices and regulatory requirements.

By implementing these strategies, pharmaceutical companies can effectively protect sensitive data, maintain regulatory compliance, and safeguard patient privacy and intellectual property.

Part 2: Implementation and Benefits

Digital Transformation Strategies for Pharma

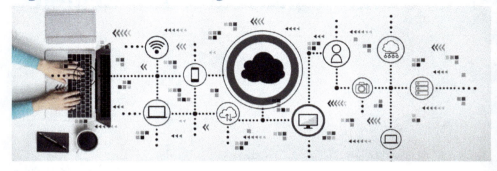

Change Management and Organizational Readiness

Change management and organizational readiness are crucial components of successful digital transformation in the pharmaceutical industry. Here's an overview of these concepts and their importance:

Change management involves a systematic approach to transitioning individuals, teams, and organizations from a current state to a desired future state. In the context of digital transformation, it includes:

1. Assessing Current State: Evaluate the organization's current digital maturity and readiness for change.
2. Defining Change Objectives: Clearly articulate the goals and benefits of digital transformation to stakeholders.
3. Developing a Change Strategy: Create a comprehensive plan for implementing changes, including timelines, resources, and communication strategies.
4. Engaging Stakeholders: Involve key stakeholders in the change process to ensure buy-in and support.
5. Training and Development: Provide necessary training to employees to adapt to new technologies and processes.

Organizational Readiness

Organizational readiness refers to the ability of an organization to successfully implement and sustain change. Key aspects include:
1. Technological Infrastructure: Assessing the organization's technology capabilities and readiness for digital transformation.
2. Business Processes: Evaluating the maturity of business processes and their alignment with digital strategies.
3. Management Capacity: Ensuring leadership is equipped to drive and support digital transformation.
4. Human Capacity: Assessing the skills and adaptability of the workforce to new technologies.
5. Corporate Culture: Fostering a culture that embraces innovation and continuous improvement.

Importance in Digital Transformation

- Enhanced Efficiency: Effective change management and organizational readiness ensure that digital transformation initiatives are implemented smoothly, minimizing disruptions and enhancing operational efficiency.
- Improved Adoption: When employees are prepared and engaged, they are more likely to adopt new technologies and processes, leading to better outcomes.
- Regulatory Compliance: Ensuring that changes are managed properly helps maintain regulatory compliance, which is critical in the pharmaceutical industry.
- Innovation and Competitiveness: Organizations that are ready for digital transformation can innovate faster and remain competitive in a rapidly evolving market.

By focusing on change management and organizational readiness, pharmaceutical companies can navigate digital transformation more effectively, ensuring that they leverage new technologies to improve patient outcomes and maintain a competitive edge.

Building a Digital Culture within Pharmaceutical Companies

Building a digital culture within pharmaceutical companies is essential for successful digital transformation. This involves fostering an environment that encourages innovation, collaboration, and continuous learning. Here are some strategies to help build a digital culture:

Strategies for Building a Digital Culture

1. Foster a Culture of Innovation:
   o Encourage experimentation and learning from failures. Provide resources and support for employees to explore new technologies and ideas.
   o Celebrate successes and recognize contributions to innovation, reinforcing a culture that values creativity and progress.
2. Develop a Digital Mindset:
   o Train employees in digital literacy and provide ongoing education in emerging technologies like AI, IoT, and cloud computing.
   o Encourage data-driven decision-making across all levels of the organization.
3. Promote Collaboration and Open Communication:
   o Implement platforms that facilitate cross-functional collaboration and open communication.
   o Use digital tools to enhance transparency and feedback loops, ensuring that all stakeholders are aligned and engaged.

4. Lead by Example:
   - Leadership should champion digital transformation and demonstrate a commitment to innovation.
   - Leaders should model the behaviors they expect from employees, such as embracing change and learning from failures.
5. Change Management and Coaching:
   - Implement change management strategies to address resistance to change.
   - Provide coaching and support to help employees adapt to new technologies and workflows.
6. Recognize and Reward Digital Achievements:
   - Implement recognition programs that reward employees for contributing to digital initiatives.
   - Use incentives to motivate employees to embrace digital transformation and suggest new ideas.

Challenges and Opportunities

- Challenges: Overcoming cultural resistance to change, ensuring digital fluency across the workforce, and maintaining a competitive edge in a rapidly evolving industry.
- Opportunities: Enhanced innovation, improved operational efficiency, and better patient outcomes through personalized treatments and streamlined drug development processes.

By focusing on these strategies, pharmaceutical companies can build a robust digital culture that supports continuous innovation and adaptation, ultimately driving success in the digital age.

Enhancing Operational Efficiency

Streamlining Production Processes with Automation

Streamlining production processes with automation in the pharmaceutical industry involves leveraging advanced technologies to enhance efficiency, quality, and compliance. Here's how automation contributes to streamlined production:

Benefits of Automation in Streamlining Production

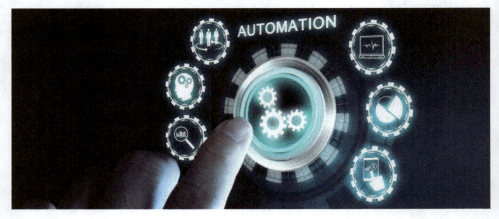

1. Increased Efficiency and Productivity:
   - Automated systems can operate continuously without breaks, significantly increasing production capacity and reducing production times.
   - Tasks that are repetitive or prone to human error are handled with precision, minimizing downtime and enhancing overall productivity.

2. Enhanced Quality Control:
    o Automation ensures consistent product quality by maintaining precise control over manufacturing processes, reducing the risk of human error.
    o Real-time monitoring and quality checks ensure that products meet the highest standards of safety and efficacy.
3. Improved Compliance:
    o Automated systems simplify compliance management by ensuring adherence to regulatory standards like GMP and providing detailed documentation.
    o This reduces the risk of non-compliance and simplifies audit processes.
4. Cost Reduction:
    o While the initial investment in automation technology can be substantial, it leads to significant cost savings over time by reducing labour costs and minimizing waste.
    o Optimized resource utilization further enhances operational efficiency.
5. Accelerated Innovation:
    o Automation frees up resources for more innovative tasks, such as accelerating drug discovery and development.
    o It enables the production of personalized medicines by streamlining processes and improving data management.

Technologies Used in Automation

1. Robotic Process Automation (RPA):
    o RPA automates repetitive tasks like data entry and labelling, reducing errors and enhancing product reliability.
2. Industrial Robots:
    o Robots excel in tasks like precise filling, medical device assembly, and packaging, ensuring consistency and accuracy at high speeds.
3. Automated Material Handling Systems:
    o These systems ensure that materials are delivered to the right place at the right time, minimizing delays and reducing waste.
4. AI and Machine Learning:
    o AI and ML enhance automation by analysing large datasets to optimize processes and predict potential issues.

By integrating these automation technologies, pharmaceutical companies can significantly streamline production processes, improve product quality, and enhance regulatory compliance while reducing costs and accelerating innovation.

Reducing Costs and Improving Productivity

Reducing costs and improving productivity in pharmaceutical manufacturing involves implementing strategic approaches and leveraging advanced technologies. Here are some key strategies and technologies that can help achieve these goals:

Strategies for Reducing Costs

1. Strategic Sourcing:
   o Optimize raw material procurement by leveraging long-term partnerships with suppliers to secure preferred pricing and quality materials.
   o Use consolidated purchasing and contract negotiation techniques to reduce costs.
2. Lean Manufacturing:
   o Apply lean principles to eliminate non-value-added activities and processes, enhancing efficiency and productivity.
   o Implement value-stream mapping and continuous improvement initiatives like Kaizen events.
3. Supply Chain Optimization:
   o Enhance production planning and inventory management to minimize stockouts and overstocking.
   o Reduce lead times and improve demand forecasting to enhance supply chain agility.
4. Yield Improvement:
   o Optimize processes and adopt technological advancements to increase yields, reducing production costs.
   o Benchmark biopharmaceutical processes and adopt best practices to improve efficiency.

Technologies for Improving Productivity

1. Automation and Robotics:
   - o Automate repetitive tasks to reduce errors and enhance efficiency.
   - o Use robotics for precise operations like filling and packaging.
2. Digital Technologies:
   - o Leverage digital instruments to reduce maintenance needs and simplify regulatory compliance.
   - o Implement AI and machine learning to optimize drug discovery and manufacturing processes.
3. Real-Time Monitoring and Analytics:
   - o Use real-time data analytics to optimize production processes and predict potential issues.
   - o Implement in-line process analytics to reduce testing time and improve quality control.
4. Pharmaceutical ERP Systems:
   - o Streamline business operations and ensure compliance with industry regulations.
   - o Manage the entire product lifecycle from development to distribution.

Benefits of Implementation

- Cost Savings: Reduced raw material costs, lower inventory levels, and minimized waste contribute to significant cost savings.
- Improved Efficiency: Automation and lean manufacturing enhance productivity, reducing production times and improving product consistency.
- Enhanced Quality: Real-time monitoring and quality control ensure consistent product quality, reducing the risk of recalls and improving patient safety.

By implementing these strategies and technologies, pharmaceutical companies can achieve substantial reductions in costs while improving productivity and maintaining high-quality standards.

Quality Control and Compliance

Using Digital Tools for Regulatory Compliance

Digital tools play a crucial role in enhancing regulatory compliance in the pharmaceutical industry by streamlining processes, reducing errors, and ensuring adherence to complex regulatory standards. Here's an overview of how digital tools support regulatory compliance:

Key Digital Tools for Regulatory Compliance

1. Electronic Document Management Systems (EDMS):
   - EDMSs efficiently store, retrieve, and manage documents required for regulatory submissions, audits, and inspections, ensuring that no document is lost or outdated.
   - They provide a centralized platform for document control, version management, and electronic signatures.

2. Automated Compliance Monitoring and Reporting:
    o AI-powered tools continuously monitor marketing assets and healthcare professional portals to flag non-compliant content, ensuring real-time compliance with promotional regulations.
    o These tools automate reporting processes, reducing manual workloads and enhancing accuracy.
3. Informatics Platforms:
    o Informatics platforms assist in managing, analysing, and reporting data to ensure compliance with GMP and GLP standards.
    o They facilitate centralized data management, ensuring data integrity and traceability throughout the drug development lifecycle.
4. Regulatory Intelligence Systems:
    o These systems help navigate the global regulatory landscape by providing updates on changing regulations and ensuring compliance across different markets.
    o They streamline product rollouts by maintaining compliance with diverse regulatory requirements.
5. Digital Collaboration Tools:
    o Virtual collaboration platforms ensure seamless communication among stakeholders, maintaining regulatory standards even in decentralized trials and remote audits.
    o They facilitate real-time feedback and continuous improvement, aligning processes with regulatory expectations.

Benefits of Digital Tools in Regulatory Compliance

- Efficiency and Accuracy: Digital tools automate repetitive tasks, reduce human errors, and streamline workflows, ensuring timely compliance with regulatory deadlines.
- Data Integrity and Traceability: Informatics platforms maintain data integrity by implementing robust security measures, audit trails, and electronic signatures.
- Real-Time Monitoring and Alerts: Digital systems provide real-time monitoring against regulatory benchmarks, enabling swift corrective actions if deviations occur.
- Global Compliance: Digital tools help navigate complex regulatory landscapes globally, ensuring compliance with diverse standards and regulations.

By leveraging these digital tools, pharmaceutical companies can enhance their regulatory compliance posture, reduce risks, and improve operational efficiency while maintaining high-quality standards and patient safety.

Ensuring Data Integrity and Traceability

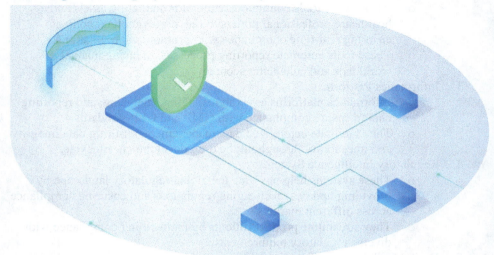

Ensuring data integrity and traceability in the pharmaceutical industry is crucial for maintaining the quality, safety, and efficacy of medicinal products. Here's an overview of how data integrity and traceability are ensured:

Ensuring Data Integrity

1. ALCOA Principles:
   o Attributable: Clearly show who observed and recorded data.
   o Legible: Easy to understand and permanent.
   o Contemporaneous: Recorded as it was observed when it was executed.
   o Original: Accessible and preserved in native form.
   o Accurate: Error-free and conforming with protocols.
   o Complete: Include an audit trail that shows nothing was lost or deleted.
   o Consistent: Displayed the same way wherever it is accessed.
   o Enduring: Accessible and readable during the entire lifecycle.
   o Available: Documents should be accessible in a readable format to required personnel.
2. Risk-Based Strategies:
   o Implement risk assessments to identify potential data integrity issues and develop strategies to mitigate these risks.
   o Use electronic systems to automate data collection and ensure audit trails for all changes.
3. Good Documentation Practices (GDPs):
   o Ensure that all data is recorded accurately and consistently, with clear documentation practices in place for manual and electronic data.

Ensuring Traceability

1. Serialization and Barcoding:
   o Use unique identifiers on each product package to enable tracking throughout the supply chain.
   o Implement centralized databases to manage and monitor these identifiers.
2. Blockchain Technology:
   o Utilize blockchain for secure and transparent data sharing across the supply chain, enhancing trust and reducing counterfeiting risks.
3. Real-Time Monitoring:
   o Implement IoT devices and sensors to track products in real-time, ensuring immediate detection of irregularities or counterfeit products.
4. Regulatory Compliance:
   o Adhere to global regulations like the European Falsified Medicines Directive (FMD) and India's traceability guidelines to ensure compliance and safety.

Benefits of Data Integrity and Traceability

- Quality and Safety: Ensures that products meet quality standards and are safe for patients.
- Regulatory Compliance: Reduces the risk of non-compliance and associated penalties.
- Efficiency and Transparency: Enhances operational efficiency and provides real-time visibility across the supply chain.
- Trust and Reputation: Builds trust with regulators, customers, and stakeholders by maintaining high standards of data integrity and traceability.

By focusing on these strategies, pharmaceutical companies can ensure the integrity of their data and the traceability of their products, ultimately contributing to patient safety and regulatory compliance.

Personalized Medicine and Patient-Centric Approaches

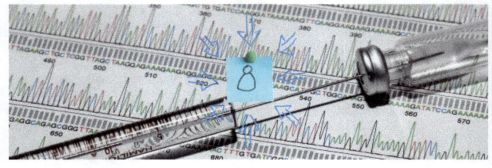

Role of Pharma 4.0 in Personalized Medicine

Pharma 4.0 plays a pivotal role in personalized medicine by leveraging advanced technologies like AI, big data analytics, and IoT to tailor treatments to individual patients' needs. Here's how Pharma 4.0 contributes to personalized medicine:

1. Data-Driven Insights:
   - Genomic Analysis: Pharma 4.0 uses AI and machine learning to analyse genomic data, predicting how patients might respond to different treatments based on their genetic profiles.
   - Real-Time Data Collection: IoT devices and digital health platforms collect real-time patient data, enabling continuous monitoring and adjustments to treatment plans.
2. Precision Therapies:
   - Targeted Treatments: Pharma 4.0 facilitates the development of targeted therapies by analysing large datasets to identify specific biomarkers and genetic mutations, ensuring treatments are more effective for individual patients.
   - Autologous Cell Therapies: Technologies like autologous cell therapy are supported by Pharma 4.0, where treatments are tailored using a patient's own cells.
3. Enhanced Patient Engagement:
   - Digital Health Platforms: Pharma 4.0 leverages digital health platforms and telemedicine services to enhance patient engagement, improve treatment adherence, and enable remote monitoring.
   - Personalized Treatment Plans: AI-driven insights help create personalized treatment plans that consider a patient's lifestyle, medical history, and genetic information.
4. Supply Chain Optimization:
   - Real-Time Tracking: IoT and blockchain technologies ensure real-time tracking and monitoring of personalized medicines throughout the supply chain, maintaining product integrity and preventing counterfeiting.

44

Benefits of Pharma 4.0 in Personalized Medicine

- Improved Treatment Efficacy: Personalized treatments lead to better patient outcomes by targeting specific genetic or molecular profiles.
- Reduced Adverse Reactions: Tailored therapies minimize the risk of adverse reactions, enhancing patient safety.
- Enhanced Patient Satisfaction: Personalized approaches improve patient engagement and satisfaction by addressing individual needs more effectively.
- Accelerated Drug Development: Pharma 4.0 technologies accelerate the development of personalized treatments by streamlining clinical trials and optimizing drug discovery processes.

By integrating these technologies, Pharma 4.0 enables the pharmaceutical industry to deliver more effective, personalized treatments, improving patient outcomes and enhancing the overall quality of care.

45

Patient-Centric Innovations enabled by Digital Technologies

Patient-centric innovations enabled by digital technologies are transforming the pharmaceutical industry by enhancing patient engagement, improving treatment outcomes, and fostering personalized care. Here are some key innovations and their benefits:

Patient-Centric Innovations

1. Digital Health Platforms:
   - Patient Engagement Tools: Platforms like Pfizer's RxPathways provide patients with educational resources, medication reminders, and wellness tips, empowering them to manage their treatments more effectively1.
   - Telemedicine Integration: Companies like Eli Lilly integrate telemedicine services to enhance access to healthcare and streamline prescription processes.
2. Personalized Medicine:
   - Data-Driven Insights: Advanced data analytics help understand patient needs on an individual basis, tailoring treatments to their unique genetic makeup, lifestyle, and medical history.
   - AI-Driven Treatment Plans: AI analyses genomic data to create personalized cancer treatment plans, as seen in AstraZeneca's collaboration with Tempus.
3. Digital Companion Apps:
   - Health Monitoring: Apps like AstraZeneca's HAYA empower patients to monitor their health and track progress, enhancing medication adherence and patient engagement.
   - Real-Time Feedback: These apps provide real-time updates to healthcare providers, enabling adjustments in treatment plans based on patient responses.
4. Wearable Devices and IoT:
   - Continuous Monitoring: Wearables like smartwatches collect biometric data continuously, providing insights into drug efficacy and patient adherence outside clinical settings.
   - Enhanced Clinical Trials: Wearable data reduces reliance on self-reported outcomes, improving trial accuracy and speeding up drug development.

Benefits of Patient-Centric Innovations

- Improved Patient Outcomes: Personalized treatments lead to better efficacy and reduced adverse effects.
- Enhanced Patient Engagement: Digital tools empower patients to take an active role in their healthcare, improving adherence and satisfaction.
- Increased Efficiency: Digital platforms streamline clinical trials and healthcare services, reducing costs and improving operational efficiency.
- Competitive Advantage: Companies adopting patient-centric innovations differentiate themselves by offering more effective and personalized care solutions.

By leveraging these digital technologies, pharmaceutical companies can deliver more effective, patient-centered care, ultimately enhancing patient satisfaction and improving health outcomes.

Part 3: Future Directions and Challenges

Future Trends in Pharma 4.0

Emerging Technologies like Blockchain and 3D Printing

Emerging technologies like blockchain and 3D printing are transforming the pharmaceutical industry by enhancing supply chain integrity, improving drug manufacturing, and enabling personalized medicine. Here's an overview of how these technologies are impacting the industry:

Blockchain Technology

1. Supply Chain Integrity:
   o Blockchain provides a secure and immutable ledger for tracking drugs throughout the supply chain, ensuring authenticity and reducing counterfeiting risks.
   o It enhances transparency and accountability by creating a tamper-proof record of transactions and product movements.
2. Regulatory Compliance:
   o Blockchain helps streamline regulatory compliance by maintaining accurate and auditable records, simplifying audits and ensuring data integrity.
   o This technology supports secure data sharing among stakeholders, facilitating collaboration and innovation in drug development.
3. Patient Data Security:
   o Blockchain can safeguard patient data by providing secure and decentralized storage solutions, enhancing privacy and trust in healthcare services.

3D Printing Technology

1. Personalized Medicine:
   - 3D printing enables the creation of customized medications tailored to individual patient needs, improving treatment efficacy and reducing side effects.
   - This technology allows for precise control over drug dosage, release profiles, and formulations, enhancing patient outcomes.
2. Flexible Manufacturing:
   - 3D printing offers flexibility in drug formulation, allowing for the rapid production of complex dosage forms that are difficult to achieve with traditional methods.
   - It supports on-demand manufacturing, reducing development time and costs associated with traditional pharmaceutical production processes.
3. Improved Patient Compliance:
   - 3D printing can create medications with customized shapes, sizes, and flavors, improving patient compliance by making drugs more palatable and easier to administer.

Future Directions

- Integration and Adoption: The future will see increased integration of blockchain and 3D printing technologies into mainstream pharmaceutical operations, enhancing supply chain security and personalized medicine capabilities.

- Regulatory Frameworks: Regulatory bodies will need to develop frameworks that support the adoption of these emerging technologies while ensuring safety and efficacy standards are maintained.
- Collaboration and Innovation: Collaboration between industry stakeholders, researchers, and regulatory bodies will be crucial for driving innovation and overcoming challenges associated with these technologies.

By leveraging blockchain and 3D printing, the pharmaceutical industry can achieve significant improvements in supply chain integrity, drug manufacturing flexibility, and personalized patient care, ultimately enhancing healthcare outcomes and patient satisfaction.

Potential Impact on Drug Development and Manufacturing

The potential impact of emerging technologies like blockchain and 3D printing on drug development and manufacturing is significant, offering improvements in efficiency, quality, and patient-centric care.

Impact of Blockchain on Drug Development and Manufacturing

1. Supply Chain Transparency and Security:
   - Blockchain enhances supply chain integrity by providing a secure and transparent ledger for tracking drugs from production to delivery, reducing counterfeiting risks and improving patient safety.
   - It streamlines regulatory compliance by maintaining accurate and auditable records, simplifying audits and ensuring data integrity.
2. Clinical Trials and Data Management:
   - Blockchain can record every step of clinical trials securely, ensuring data integrity and transparency in participant recruitment, data collection, and analysis.
   - This technology automates crucial operations and strengthens pharmaceutical product integrity using smart contracts and decentralized apps.
3. Reduced Intermediaries and Costs:
   - Blockchain reduces the number of intermediaries involved in the pharmaceutical process, lowering costs and improving efficiency.

Impact of 3D Printing on Drug Development and Manufacturing

1. Personalized Medicine:
    - o 3D printing enables the creation of customized medications tailored to individual patient needs, improving treatment efficacy and reducing side effects.
    - o It allows for precise control over drug dosage, release profiles, and formulations, enhancing patient outcomes.
2. On-Demand Manufacturing:
    - o 3D printing facilitates on-demand, prescription-specific production, which is particularly beneficial for emergency medicine and medications with limited shelf-life.
    - o This approach reduces development time and costs associated with traditional manufacturing processes.
3. Complex Drug Structures:
    - o 3D printing allows for the fabrication of complex drug structures with precise control over release characteristics, offering flexibility not available with traditional methods.

By integrating blockchain and 3D printing into drug development and manufacturing, pharmaceutical companies can enhance supply chain security, improve product customization, and accelerate innovation, ultimately leading to better patient outcomes and more efficient drug development processes.

Challenges and Limitations

Addressing Regulatory Hurdles and Cybersecurity Risks

Addressing regulatory hurdles and cybersecurity risks in the pharmaceutical industry involves a multifaceted approach that includes proactive compliance strategies, robust cybersecurity measures, and continuous monitoring. Here's an overview of how to address these challenges:

Addressing Regulatory Hurdles

1. Engage with Regulatory Bodies Early:
   o Engage with regulatory agencies early in the drug development process to understand requirements and expectations, reducing the risk of costly delays or rejections.
   o Regularly seek guidance and feedback from regulators to ensure compliance with evolving standards.
2. Leverage Regulatory Expertise:
   o Build or access regulatory expertise by hiring experienced professionals or consulting with regulatory affairs experts.
   o Stay informed about regulatory changes and trends to adapt strategies as needed.

3. Integrated Compliance Frameworks:
   o Implement integrated compliance frameworks that connect all organizational areas, ensuring a holistic view of compliance.
   o Streamline compliance activities by coordinating quality management, risk management, and regulatory requirements across departments.
4. Regulatory Intelligence Tools:
   o Use regulatory intelligence tools to track developments and anticipate changes in regulatory standards.
   o Stay updated on emerging regulatory practices to proactively adjust compliance strategies.

Addressing Cybersecurity Risks

1. Implement Advanced Security Controls:
   o Establish stringent security controls, including advanced encryption protocols, multi-factor authentication, and frequent software updates.
   o Use secure network segmentation to safeguard sensitive data.
2. Regular Cybersecurity Risk Assessments:
   o Conduct proactive cybersecurity risk assessments to identify vulnerabilities and strengthen infrastructure.
   o Evaluate third-party vendors and supply chain partners to mitigate risks.
3. Employee Training and Awareness:
   o Invest in cybersecurity training programs to educate employees on best practices and phishing attack identification.
   o Encourage a culture of security awareness to prevent human error-related breaches.
4. Secure Software Development:
   o Implement secure software development practices for medical devices and software used in pharmaceutical operations.
   o Ensure that all software is designed with security in mind to protect patient data and intellectual property.

By adopting these strategies, pharmaceutical companies can effectively navigate regulatory hurdles and mitigate cybersecurity risks, ensuring compliance, protecting sensitive data, and maintaining public trust.

Overcoming Cultural and Technological Barriers

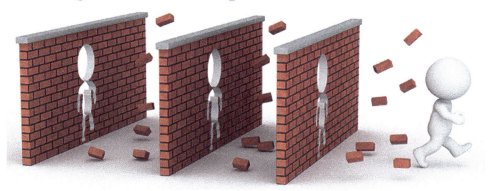

Overcoming cultural and technological barriers in the pharmaceutical industry involves a multifaceted approach that addresses both the cultural nuances of diverse teams and the technological challenges of digital transformation. Here's an overview of strategies to overcome these barriers:

Overcoming Cultural Barriers

1. Cultural Competency Training:
   o Provide training for leaders and employees to enhance cultural sensitivity and understanding, fostering a more inclusive workplace environment.
   o Encourage empathy and respect for diverse backgrounds, improving communication and collaboration across teams.
2. Effective Communication:
   o Implement clear and transparent communication strategies that consider language and cultural differences.
   o Use interpreters or multilingual tools when necessary to ensure that all stakeholders understand critical information.
3. Inclusive Leadership:
   o Leaders should model inclusive behaviors, promoting fairness and equal opportunities for all employees.
   o Encourage cross-cultural collaboration by celebrating cultural differences and promoting understanding.
4. Employee Engagement:
   o Involve employees in decision-making processes to foster a sense of ownership and trust.
   o Address employee concerns openly to build trust and reduce resistance to change.

Overcoming Technological Barriers

1. Digital Literacy Training:
   - Offer comprehensive training programs to enhance employees' digital skills, ensuring they can effectively use new technologies.
   - Provide ongoing support and resources to help employees adapt to evolving digital tools.
2. Technology Integration:
   - Gradually integrate new technologies into existing systems, ensuring seamless transitions and minimizing disruptions.
   - Use agile methodologies to quickly adapt to technological changes and improve system flexibility.
3. Cybersecurity Measures:
   - Implement robust cybersecurity measures to protect sensitive data and maintain trust in digital systems.
   - Regularly update security protocols to address emerging threats and ensure compliance with regulatory standards.
4. Collaboration with IT Teams:
   - Work closely with IT teams to address technical issues promptly and ensure that digital solutions meet business needs.
   - Foster a culture of innovation, encouraging feedback and suggestions from employees on how to improve technological processes.

By addressing both cultural and technological barriers, pharmaceutical companies can create a more inclusive and technologically adept environment, enhancing collaboration, innovation, and overall operational efficiency.

Case Studies and Success Stories

Real-world examples of Pharma 4.0 implementation

Here are some real-world examples of Pharma 4.0 implementation:

1. Johnson & Johnson's Pharma 4.0 Implementation:
   - Johnson & Johnson has seen significant benefits from implementing Pharma 4.0 technologies, including a 50% reduction in unplanned downtime, a 4.5 percentage point increase in OTIF scores, and a 90% decrease in product development testing lead times.
2. Novartis and Eli Lilly's Digital Transformation:
   - Both companies have embarked on digital transformation journeys, leveraging platforms like Aizon for advanced analytics to enhance manufacturing processes. Novartis and Eli Lilly have presented their experiences at ISPE meetings, highlighting the adoption of Pharma 4.0 technologies.
3. Sterile Pharma CDMO Case Study:
   - A sterile pharma CDMO implemented Pharma 4.0 solutions to enhance visibility and productivity. By actively monitoring production lines, they reduced downtime by 30%, demonstrating the potential of digital technologies to improve operational efficiency.
4. Novo Nordisk's Adoption of Aizon Platform:
   - Novo Nordisk, one of the world's largest insulin manufacturers, has adopted the Aizon advanced analytics platform as part of their digital transformation. This platform supports Pharma 4.0 initiatives by enhancing manufacturing processes through data-driven insights.
5. Electronic Logbooks and Line Clearance:
   - Companies are using electronic logbooks and digital line clearance applications to streamline manual processes, improve data integrity, and enhance process visibility. These tools ensure compliance with ALCOA principles and facilitate efficient line transfers.

These examples illustrate how Pharma 4.0 technologies are being applied in real-world settings to improve efficiency, quality, and innovation in pharmaceutical manufacturing.

Lessons learned from early adopters

Early adopters of Pharma 4.0 have provided valuable lessons that can guide other companies in their digital transformation journey. Here are some key insights:

1. Emphasize Digital Maturity Assessment:
    o   Early adopters highlight the importance of assessing digital maturity before implementing Pharma 4.0 technologies. This assessment helps identify areas for improvement and ensures that the organization is ready for digital transformation.
2. Address Regulatory Uncertainties:
    o   Companies like Johnson & Johnson have shown that engaging with regulatory bodies early in the process can mitigate risks associated with new technologies. This proactive approach helps ensure compliance with evolving standards.
3. Invest in Cybersecurity:
    o   Given the increased reliance on digital systems, cybersecurity is a critical concern. Early adopters stress the need for robust security measures to protect sensitive data and maintain operational continuity.
4. Foster a Culture of Innovation:
    o   Successful implementation of Pharma 4.0 requires a culture that embraces change and innovation. Companies must invest in employee training and encourage a mindset that supports continuous improvement.
5. Collaborate with Technology Partners:
    o   Partnering with technology providers can help navigate the complexities of digital transformation. This collaboration is essential for integrating new technologies seamlessly into existing systems.

6. Focus on Data Governance:
   o Effective data management is crucial for leveraging Pharma 4.0 technologies. Early adopters emphasize the need for strong data governance practices to ensure data integrity and compliance.
7. Monitor and Adapt to Technological Advancements:
   o The pharmaceutical industry is rapidly evolving, with new technologies emerging continuously. Early adopters must stay informed about the latest advancements and adapt their strategies accordingly.

By learning from these experiences, pharmaceutical companies can better navigate the challenges of digital transformation and maximize the benefits of Pharma 4.0 technologies.

Conclusion

Conclusion

Vision for the Future of Pharmaceutical Manufacturing

The future of pharmaceutical manufacturing is envisioned as a highly integrated and technologically advanced sector, driven by the principles of Pharma 4.0. Here's a vision for this future:

Vision for the Future of Pharmaceutical Manufacturing

1. Digital Transformation and Automation:
   - Smart Factories: Manufacturing facilities will become "smart factories" where digital technologies like AI, IoT, and blockchain are fully integrated to enhance efficiency, quality, and compliance.
   - Real-Time Monitoring: Real-time monitoring and predictive analytics will be used to optimize production processes, reduce downtime, and ensure consistent product quality.
2. Personalized Medicine:
   - Tailored Treatments: The industry will focus on developing personalized treatments using advanced data analytics and genomics, improving patient outcomes by tailoring drugs to individual genetic profiles.
   - Mass Customization: Manufacturing processes will be reconfigured to support mass customization of personalized medications, leveraging technologies like 3D printing.

3. Supply Chain Resilience:
   - o Enhanced Visibility: Supply chains will be optimized using digital technologies to enhance visibility, reduce risks, and ensure timely delivery of critical medications.
   - o Sustainable Practices: Companies will adopt sustainable manufacturing practices to reduce environmental impact while maintaining operational efficiency.
4. Regulatory Compliance and Security:
   - o Regulatory Alignment: The industry will align with evolving regulatory standards, ensuring compliance while adopting new technologies.
   - o Cybersecurity Measures: Robust cybersecurity measures will be implemented to protect sensitive data and maintain system security in a highly interconnected environment.
5. Global Collaboration and Innovation:
   - o International Partnerships: Pharmaceutical companies will engage in global partnerships to accelerate innovation, leveraging diverse expertise and resources.
   - o Emerging Markets: There will be increased focus on emerging markets like India, which are poised for significant growth in pharmaceutical manufacturing and innovation.

By embracing these trends, the pharmaceutical industry can achieve a future where manufacturing is more efficient, personalized, and responsive to patient needs, while maintaining high standards of quality and regulatory compliance.

Call to Action for Industry Stakeholders

Here's a call to action for industry stakeholders in the pharmaceutical sector:
Embracing the Future of Pharmaceutical Manufacturing: A Call to Action
As we navigate the transformative landscape of Pharma 4.0, it is crucial for industry stakeholders to collaborate and innovate together. Here are key actions to drive forward this vision:

For Pharmaceutical Companies

1. Invest in Digital Transformation:
   - Leverage technologies like AI, IoT, and blockchain to enhance manufacturing efficiency, quality control, and supply chain transparency.
   - Implement pilot projects to test new technologies and scale successful initiatives across the organization.
2. Foster Stakeholder Engagement:
   - Engage with patients, healthcare providers, and regulators to ensure that products meet real-world needs and comply with regulatory standards.
   - Use feedback from stakeholders to improve drug development processes and enhance patient outcomes.
3. Promote a Culture of Innovation:
   - Encourage continuous learning and innovation within your organization, focusing on emerging technologies and their applications in pharmaceutical manufacturing.
   - Support employee training programs to enhance digital literacy and adaptability.

For Regulators

1. Provide Clear Regulatory Guidance:
    - Develop and communicate clear guidelines for the adoption of new technologies in pharmaceutical manufacturing.
    - Engage with industry stakeholders to ensure that regulatory frameworks support innovation while maintaining safety and efficacy standards.
2. Encourage Patient-Centric Approaches:
    - Support initiatives that involve patients in drug development and evaluation processes, ensuring that treatments meet patient needs effectively.
    - Foster collaboration between regulators, industry, and patient groups to enhance regulatory processes.

For Patients and Patient Advocacy Groups

1. Engage in Drug Development Processes:
    - Participate in initiatives like EUPATI to provide meaningful input into drug development and evaluation.
    - Advocate for patient-centric approaches that prioritize real-world needs and outcomes.
2. Collaborate with Industry Partners:
    - Work with pharmaceutical companies to ensure that products are designed with patient needs in mind.
    - Use platforms like CTTI to enhance patient involvement in clinical trials and regulatory discussions.

For Technology Providers

1. Develop Solutions Aligned with Industry Needs:
    - Collaborate with pharmaceutical companies to understand their challenges and develop tailored solutions that enhance operational efficiency and product quality.
    - Ensure that technologies are designed with regulatory compliance and patient safety in mind.
2. Support Innovation and Scalability:
    - Provide scalable solutions that can adapt to the evolving needs of the pharmaceutical industry.
    - Encourage the adoption of emerging technologies like blockchain and AI to drive innovation.

By working together, industry stakeholders can accelerate the adoption of Pharma 4.0 technologies, enhance patient outcomes, and drive sustainable growth in the pharmaceutical sector.

Appendix

Glossary of key terms

1. Pharma 4.0:
   - The integration of Industry 4.0 technologies into pharmaceutical manufacturing to enhance efficiency, quality, and innovation.
2. Artificial Intelligence (AI):
   - Technologies that enable machines to perform tasks that typically require human intelligence, such as learning and problem-solving.
3. Internet of Things (IoT):
   - The network of physical devices, vehicles, home appliances, and other items embedded with sensors, software, and connectivity, allowing them to collect and exchange data.
4. Blockchain:
   - A decentralized, digital ledger that records transactions across a network of computers, ensuring data integrity and transparency.
5. 3D Printing:
   - A manufacturing process that creates products by layering materials such as metals, plastics, and ceramics, enabling rapid prototyping and personalized production.
6. Machine Learning (ML):
   - A subset of AI that involves training algorithms to learn from data and make predictions or decisions without being explicitly programmed.
7. Cloud Computing:
   - A model for delivering computing services over the internet, providing on-demand access to a shared pool of configurable computing resources.
8. Big Data Analytics:
   - The process of examining large data sets to gain insights, uncover hidden patterns, and make informed decisions.
9. Digital Transformation:
   - The integration of digital technology into all areas of a business, fundamentally changing how it operates and delivers value to customers.
10. Personalized Medicine:
    - An approach to medical treatment that involves tailoring treatments to individual patients based on their unique genetic profiles, lifestyle, and medical history.
11. Regulatory Compliance:
    - The adherence to laws, regulations, and standards that govern the pharmaceutical industry, ensuring safety, efficacy, and quality of products.
12. Cybersecurity:
    - Practices and technologies designed to protect digital information, networks, and systems from unauthorized access, use, disclosure, disruption, modification, or destruction.

13. Smart Manufacturing:
    o The integration of advanced technologies like AI, IoT, and robotics into manufacturing processes to enhance efficiency, quality, and flexibility.
14. Quality Control (QC):
    o Processes and procedures designed to ensure that products meet specified quality standards, involving testing and inspection to detect and correct defects.
15. Supply Chain Management:
    o The coordination and management of activities involved in sourcing and procuring raw materials, transforming them into intermediate and finished goods, and delivering them to customers.

By understanding these terms, stakeholders can better navigate the complexities of Pharma 4.0 and contribute to its ongoing development and adoption in the pharmaceutical industry.

Resources for further learning

1. News-Medical.net:
   o Offers articles and insights into Pharma 4.0, including its impact on pharmaceutical manufacturing and drug development.
2. PDA Bookstore:
   o Provides books and resources on digital transformation and regulatory considerations for biopharmaceutical and healthcare manufacturers.
3. IPI Academy:
   o Offers courses and training sessions on Pharma 4.0, focusing on smart technologies and digital transformation strategies.
4. SCW.AI:
   o Provides guides and insights on modernizing pharmaceutical factories with Pharma 4.0 technologies, enhancing efficiency and innovation.
5. Westbourne IT:
   o Offers expertise and resources on digital transformation in the pharmaceutical industry, including process optimization and compliance.
6. Synthesis Solutions:
   o Discusses the role of Pharma 4.0 in employee training and manufacturing automation, highlighting its benefits in resource management.
7. Apprentice.io:
   o Explains Pharma 4.0 and its implementation, focusing on advanced technologies like AI and machine learning.
8. Innopharma Education:
   o Offers educational programs and courses on Industry 4.0 and Pharma 4.0, focusing on digital transformation in life sciences.

These resources provide a comprehensive overview of Pharma 4.0 and its applications, offering insights into technological advancements, regulatory considerations, and strategic implementation

About the Author

Dr Jayant Joshi, has Engineering and Management background with more than 45 years of experience.

His passion is **Adoption of Technologies to achieve Operational and Business Excellence**.

During his long career, he has designed, developed and implemented Management and Technology Enterprise solutions with Large and Mid- size companies from Strategy to Audit / Validation to Achieve remarkable performance improvements.

He operates a **YouTube channel** named **CENTER OF EXCELLENCE PHARMA 4.0.** This channel has more than 300 videos focused on Emerging Technologies, Digital Transformation and Pharma 4.0.

These videos have depth from Strategy, Roadmap, Implementation, Change Management to Audits and Validations.

Users can access it through the following link:

https://www.youtube.com/@COE-PHARMA4.0

Additionally, Dr. Jayant Joshi offers a **comprehensive course on Udemy** called **SMART MANUFACTURING IN PHARMA**.

This course provides an in-depth exploration of Smart Manufacturing principles and technologies applied in the pharmaceutical sector, covering digitalization, automation, and data-driven decision-making to enhance efficiency, quality, and compliance.

Participants can find the course at:

https://www.udemy.com/course/smart-manufacturing-in-pharma/

Dr. Jayant Joshi also runs a **Podcast** titled **Center of Excellence - Pharma 4.**0 which explores Smart Manufacturing principles and technologies within the pharmaceutical sector.

The podcast covers how digitalization, automation, and data-driven decision-making are enhancing efficiency, quality, and compliance in pharmaceutical manufacturing processes. It caters to professionals in pharmaceuticals, technology, and those interested in the future of healthcare or pharmaceutical manufacturing.

Access the podcast here:

https://pharma4coe.podbean.com

He can be reached at

LINKEDIN

https://www.linkedin.com/in/jayantjoshi/

WEBSITE

https://respa.com

FACEBOOK

https://www.facebook.com/jayant.joshi.1422

TWITTER / X

https://x.com/jayantbjoshi

www.ingramcontent.com/pod-product-compliance
Lightning Source LLC
Chambersburg PA
CBHW071028050326
40689CB00014B/3571